Contents

Age-Appropriate Skills

Language

- following directions
- story comprehension
- descriptive and comparative language
- rhyming
- categorization
- letter and sound recognition
- statements and questions
- auditory and visual memory
- left to right tracking
- oral language
- vocabulary and concept development
- sequencing
- color words

Math

- counting to 20
- patterning
- numeral recognition
- geometric shapes
- ordinal numbers
- beginning computation
- one-to-one matching
- graphing
- measurement

Circle-Time Books

 Making Circle-Time Books ....

Follow these simple directions to assemble a circle-time book for each of the five sections of *My World*.

- Tear out and laminate the color story pages for each circle-time book.

- Bind the books with binder rings or an alternative binding method.

- Read the circle-time book as the opening activity for each section of *My World*.

Place the book on an easel or chalkboard stand and flip the pages for easy reading.

 Sharing Circle-Time Books ....

Each circle-time story introduces the topic of that section. Begin by reading the story to the children several times. The first time you read it, you might ask children to predict what the story will be about by looking at the cover illustration. In subsequent readings, use strategies such as:

- moving your finger under words as you read to model left to right tracking

- allowing children to "read" the predictable text

- asking children to identify objects in the pictures

- talking about any rhyming words

- asking children to predict what will happen next in the story

- asking questions to help children recall story details

- asking at least one question that relates to children's own lives

Circle-Time Books

"Amazing Me" (pages 13–22)
Use this colorful book to introduce children to the unit on self-discovery. Pause on each page and discuss the illustrations. Encourage children to imitate the actions performed by the child in the illustrations. Explain to children that they will be learning about themselves as individuals, as well as about families, friends, homes, and neighborhoods.

Ask questions such as:

- What does *amazing* mean? Why does the child think she is amazing?
- What are some amazing things that you can do with your body?
- Tell about a time when you helped someone do something.
- Do you think that you are amazing? Tell why or why not.

Section Two
All About My Family

"Families Are Special" (pages 51–60)
This book introduces children to the concept of family and the activities that families do together. Emphasize that each person has a family, but not all families are the same. Encourage children to talk about their own family members and what they enjoy doing together.

Ask questions such as:

- What does Jimmy do with each of his family members?
- How many people are there in Jimmy's family in all?
- Which activity mentioned in the story do you most like to do with your family?
- How is your family like the family in the story? How is it different?

Section Three
All About My Friends

"My Friends" (pages 87–96)
This delightful story teaches children about the meaning of friends. Children learn that friends are people with whom you laugh, play, eat, share, and talk. Friends also take turns and help each other. Emphasize that friends do not all look alike and that it is important to have good friends, as well as to be a good friend to others.

Ask questions such as:

- Why did the child feel alone at the beginning of the story?
- Tell about a time when you felt alone.
- What did the child do with her new friends at school?
- What makes a person a good friend?
- Do you think that good friends can disagree? Tell why or why not.

Circle-Time Books

Section Four
All About My Home

"Hide-and-Seek" (pages 125–134)
This playful story introduces children to the names of rooms within a house and daily living activities that are usually performed in each room. Emphasize that there are different kinds of houses and that not all houses are the same. Mention that animals have homes, too. While reading, encourage children to look for the hidden child in each room.

Ask questions such as:

- How do you play hide-and-seek? Have you ever played the game in your house?
- Who was hiding under the bed?
- What are the names of the rooms mentioned in the story?
- How is your house like the one in the story? How is it different?
- Where do you think the child was hiding? Tell why.

Section Five
All About My Neighborhood

"My Neighborhood" (pages 159–168)
This story teaches children about the concept of a neighborhood and the many people who live and work together there. Emphasize that neighborhoods can be different and that each person within a neighborhood helps to make it a special place in which to live.

Ask questions such as:

- Who are the people in the neighborhood?
- What does each person do to help the community?
- Name the places mentioned in the neighborhood. Tell what you can do there.
- If you could visit one of these places, which would you choose? Tell why.
- Are pets and things part of a neighborhood? Tell why or why not.
- How is your neighborhood similar to the one in the story? How is it different?

Take-Home Books

Use these simple directions to make reproducible take-home books for each of the five sections of *My World*.

1. Reproduce the book pages for each child.

2. Cut the pages along the cut lines.

3. Place the pages in order, or this may be done as a sequencing activity with children. Guide children in assembling the book page by page.

4. Staple the book together.

After making each take-home book, review the story as children turn the pages of their own books. Send the storybook home along with the Parent Letter on page 5.

Dear Parent(s) or Guardian(s),

As part of our unit *My World*, I will be presenting five storybooks with themes related to self, family, friends, homes, and neighborhoods to the class. Your child will receive a take-home storybook for you to share. Remember that reading to children helps them develop a love of reading. Regularly reading aloud to children has proven to enhance a variety of early language skills, including:

- vocabulary and concept development,
- letter recognition,
- phonemic awareness,
- auditory and visual discrimination, and
- left to right tracking.

I hope you enjoy sharing these stories with your child.

As you read to your child, remember to:

1. speak clearly and with interest.
2. track words by moving your finger under each word as you read it.
3. ask your child to help you identify objects in the pictures. Talk about these objects together.
4. discuss your own experiences as they relate to the story.
5. allow your child to express his or her own thoughts and ideas and to ask you questions.

I hope you enjoy all five of these stories.

Sincerely,

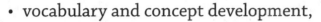

5

Storyboards

A storyboard is an excellent way to enhance vocabulary and concept development.

Each section of *My World* includes full-color storyboard pieces to use in extending the language and concepts introduced. Ideas for using the storyboard pieces in each section are found on pages 7–9.

Turn the full-color cutouts into pieces that will adhere to a flannel- or felt-covered storyboard. Just laminate the pieces and affix self-sticking Velcro® dots to the back of each piece.

All About Me
pages 29 and 31

All About My Family
pages 67 and 69

All About My Friends
pages 103 and 105

All About My Home
pages 141 and 143

All About My Neighborhood
pages 175 and 177

Storyboards

"Amazing Me" Storyboard Use the colorful storyboard pieces on pages 29 and 31 to follow up your presentation of the story "Amazing Me." You may choose to use the following teacher script to present the story:

Today we are going to learn about things we can do that make us special. I am going to show you some pictures of a child who is doing different movements with her body. As I show you each picture, I want you to tell me what the child is doing and which part of her body she is using. Then, I would like you to show me how to do the movement with your own body. Are you ready? Let's begin.

Look carefully at the first movement picture. What is the child doing in this picture? Which body part(s) is she using? Let me see you do that movement. Here is the second picture. What is the child doing in this picture? What part(s) of her body is she using now? Show me how you can move like the girl.

Continue until all storyboard pieces have been placed on the board.

As an extension, students may be paired together and asked to teach their partner a new movement. Partners may then teach the new movements to the whole class. They will use language to describe their movements.

Remove the storyboard pieces and allow children to replace each piece as they retell the story.

"Families Are Special" Storyboard Use the colorful storyboard pieces on pages 67 and 69 for your presentation of the story "Families Are Special." Place the storyboard pieces on the board one at a time in the order in which they appear in the story. You may choose to use the following teacher script to present the story:

Today we are going to review the members of Jimmy's family. Place a label on the storyboard. *This word says "father."* Point to the storyboard piece of Jimmy's father. *Let's place the storyboard piece of Jimmy's father under the word that says "father."*

This word says "mother." Point to the storyboard piece of Jimmy's mother. *Let's place the storyboard piece of Jimmy's mother under the word that says "mother."*

Continue to place all the labels and corresponding storyboard pieces on the board. Once you have completed this, ask children to tell you about which types of things Jimmy did with each family member.

Remove the storyboard pieces and allow children to replace each piece as they retell the story.

Storyboards

"My Friends" Storyboard After reading the story, have children retell the story using the storyboard pieces on pages 103 and 105. You may choose to use the following teacher script to present the story:

Today we read a story called "My Friends." Let's use the storyboard pieces to retell the story. Find the storyboard piece that shows what happened first in the story and place it on the board. *Tell us what it shows.*

Who knows what happened next? Find the storyboard piece that shows what happened next and place it next on the storyboard. *Tell us what it shows.* Repeat the process until the entire story has been retold and all storyboard pieces are displayed on the board.

Place the storyboard and pieces where children can use them independently or with a partner for more fun with the concept of friends.

Remove the storyboard pieces and allow children to replace each piece as they retell the story.

"Hide-and-Seek" Storyboard Use the colorful storyboard pieces on pages 141 and 143 to follow up your presentation of the story "Hide-and-Seek." You may choose to use the following teacher script to present the story:

Let's use our storyboard pieces to talk about some of the rooms in a house. This word says "kitchen." Place the word "kitchen" and the kitchen scene on the board and ask: *What is the name of this room? What things do you see that tell you it is a kitchen? Name some things you can do in the kitchen.* Place the word "bedroom" and the child's bedroom scene on the board and ask: *What is the name of this next room? What things do you see that tell you it is a child's bedroom? Name some things you do in your bedroom.* Continue until all rooms are displayed on the storyboard and have been discussed.

Remove the storyboard pieces and allow children to replace each piece as they retell the story.

Storyboards

"My Neighborhood" Storyboard Use the colorful storyboard pieces on pages 175 and 177 before your presentation of the story "My Neighborhood." You may choose to use the following teacher script to preview the story. Begin by placing the first piece of the child on the board and saying:

Today we are going to go on a special walk through a neighborhood. Whom do you think we might meet there?

After students predict, place each subsequent storyboard label and piece on the board and discuss what each person's job is: *Which community helper do we see in this picture? Yes, a policeman. This word says "policeman." What does this person do to help the community?*

After all storyboard pieces are displayed on the board, ask students if they can think of other examples of community helpers.

Remove the storyboard pieces and allow children to replace each piece as they retell the story.

Creating an Atmosphere

Create a delightful environment in your classroom that encourages children to be aware of their world. Make a bulletin board that lists the elements of a child's world that this theme unit will cover: me, my family, my friends, my home, and my neighborhood. Include a library center near the bulletin board where you can display books you use in this unit.

Simple Steps to Show You How

Head

Add the facial details with markers.

Hands

Make 2.

Shirt

Pants/stripes on shirt

Socks

Add red polka dots.

Shoes

Add the details with markers.

Hair

Bend and fold to create the look of tousled hair.

Background
- Staple a colorful butcher paper background to the board.

Child
- Cut the image of the child from construction paper as shown. Add details with markers.

Labels
- Cut rectangles in graduated sizes from white construction paper. Print the elements students will study in this unit on the labels.

me

family

friends

home

neighborhood

- Staple the labels to the board.

All About Me

Children learn about themselves as individuals as well as how they are alike and how they are different from each other. They learn about some of their body parts and how they use their senses.

Amazing Me

I am amazing in what I can do!

I can open and shut.
I can sing and chew.

I can clap or snap
Or move and wiggle,

Reach high or down low.
When I wink, I giggle.

4

Be as still as a mouse,
Or sniff with my nose.

I am amazing in what I can do!

Your body's like mine,
So you can learn, too.

The End

Note: Teachers will make copies and cut n half for minibooks.

Reproducible Story

Amazing Me

I am amazing
in what I can do!

1

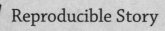

I can open and shut.
I can sing and chew.

2

I can clap or snap
Or move and wiggle,

3

Reach high or down low.

When I wink, I giggle.

4

I skip in a circle,

Stand up on tiptoes,

5

Be as still as a mouse,
Or sniff with my nose.

6

I am amazing
in what I can do!

7

Your body's like mine,
So you can learn, too.

8

The End

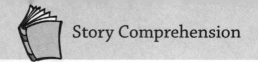
Name _____

Things I Can Do

Color the pictures from the story.

sing

reach low

play

clap

Note: See page 7 for suggestions on using the storyboard pieces on pages 29 and 31 for Amazing Me.

Storyboard Pieces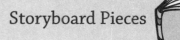

All About Me

All About Me

All About Me

All About Me

All About Me

All About Me

All About Me

All About Me

Children color, cut, and glue a book together about themselves.

Materials

- pages 34–36, reproduced, one per child

- 8 ½" x 11" (21.5 x 28 cm) construction paper

- markers or crayons

- yarn, buttons, glitter, fabric

- stapler

All About Me

Preparation

1. Fold a piece of 8 ½" x 11" (21.5 x 28 cm) construction paper to make the book cover.

2. Provide various art materials such as yarn, buttons, glitter, and fabric to decorate the cover.

3. Ask children to name a few things they like doing and that they are good at.

4. Plan time to model the steps for this project and a completed All About Me book.

Steps to Follow

1. Children color and cut out the cover on page 34. They glue it to the folded construction paper cover. Then they decorate the cover using various art materials.

2. Children color and cut out the sentence starters on pages 34 and 35.

3. Then children color and cut out the pictures on page 36 to complete each sentence. They may wish to write the name of the picture they chose on the line provided (younger children may use invented spelling).

4. Children place the pages in their book and ask an adult to staple it together.

Extension

Children may wish to glue a picture of themselves to the cover of the booklet.

Art Activity Pattern Pieces

Note: Reproduce these patterns to use with All About Me art activity.

All About Me

_____

Name

I can

_____

glue

All About My World • EMC 2403 • ©2005 by Evan-Moor Corp.

Note: Reproduce these patterns to use with All About Me art activity.

Art Activity Pattern Pieces

I like

_____

glue

I am good at

_____

glue

Note: Reproduce these patterns to use with All About Me art activity.

I can

I like

I am good at

Note: Check for allergies before beginning any cooking activity.
An allergic reaction can occur through taste, smell, or contact with allergens.

Cooking Activity

Funny Face Sandwiches

Children use healthy ingredients to prepare sandwiches that resemble faces.

Materials

- English muffin half or rice cake for each child
- paper plates
- towels
- plastic spoons
- knife (adult use only)
- variety of food items

  hair: shredded cheese, parsley, alfalfa sprouts, cereal

  eyes: raisins, grapes, sliced black olives, round cereal

  nose: strawberry, carrot, pretzel rod

  mouth: orange slice, green pepper slice, pimento

  ears: potato slices, cucumber slices, pieces of broccoli, potato chips

- "glue" to hold food items in place on the faces: butter, yogurt, soft cream cheese, or peanut butter

Preparation

1. Clean and cut fruits and vegetables.
2. Place individual food items on paper plates.
3. Discuss parts of a face. Show children which ingredients will be used for the facial features, but allow for individual creativity.
4. Plan time to model a completed Funny Face Sandwich.

Steps to Follow

1. Children place a rice cake or English muffin on a plate.
2. Then they spread "glue" (butter, yogurt, cream cheese, or peanut butter) on the muffin or rice cake.
3. Children use various ingredients to create facial features on the rice cake or English muffin.
4. Enjoy!

Extension

Allow each child to tell the class one ingredient he or she used to create a facial feature.

Dear Parent(s) or Guardian(s),

Today we cooked in class. Your child prepared a "Funny Face Sandwich." Besides having fun cooking and eating, the children practiced these skills:

- listening to and following directions
- vocabulary and concept development
- using small motor skills

For our unit *My World*, we will send home a variety of new recipes. Each recipe will be one that your child has tried in class and is excited about. We hope you have an opportunity to try this recipe again with your child. Allowing your child to help you in the kitchen is a wonderful way to reinforce learning skills while creating family memories.

Funny Face Sandwiches

Materials

- English muffin half or rice cake
- paper plates
- towels
- plastic spoons
- knife (adult use only)
- **hair:** shredded cheese, parsley, alfalfa sprouts, cereal
- **eyes:** raisins, grapes, sliced black olives, round cereal
- **nose:** strawberry, carrot, pretzel rod
- **mouth:** orange slice, green pepper slice, pimento
- **ears:** potato slices, cucumber slices, pieces of broccoli, potato chips
- "glue" to hold food items in place on the faces: butter, yogurt, soft cream cheese, or peanut butter

Steps to Follow

1. Clean and cut fruits and vegetables.
2. Place individual food items on paper plates.
3. Place a rice cake or English muffin on a plate.
4. Spread "glue" on the muffin or rice cake.
5. Use various ingredients to add facial features to the rice cake or English muffin.

Name _____

Which Body Part?

Color the body part in each row.

ABC Language—Auditory Discrimination

Note: Review the names of the pictures in each row. Children color the picture that rhymes with the first picture in each row.

Name _____

Rhyming Me!

Color the picture in each row that rhymes with the first picture.

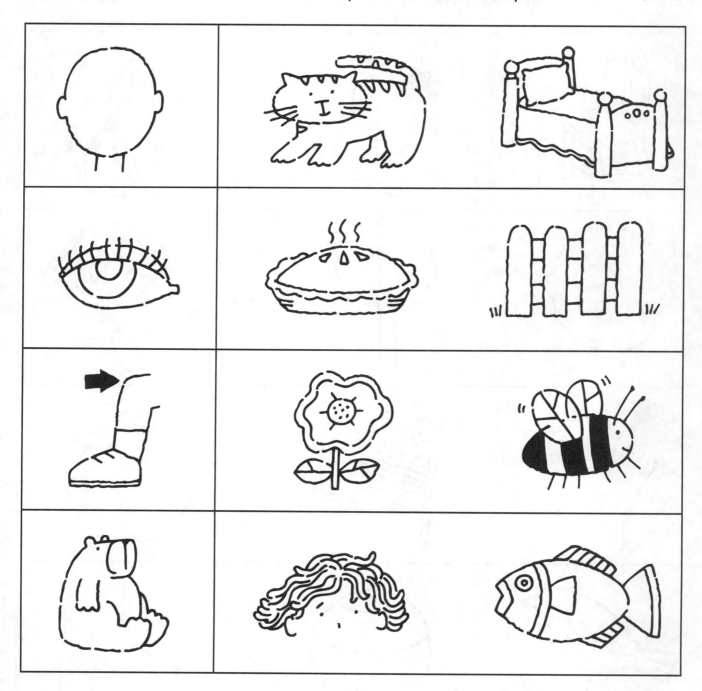

Name _____

Count

Write a number in each note.

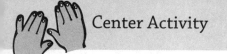

Using My Senses

Creating the Center

1. Laminate and cut out pages 43 and 45.
2. Store the cards in a sturdy folder or envelope.
3. Plan time to model how the center is used.

Using the Center

1. Show children the task cards that represent the five senses: **sight, hearing, smell, touch,** and **taste.** Discuss the ways that people use their five senses.
2. Children match each stimulus card with its correct sense card.

Children discover more about themselves through an investigation of their five senses.

Materials

- pages 43 and 45
- scissors
- sturdy folder or envelope

Using My Senses

©2005 by Evan-Moor Corp.
All About My World • EMC 2403

Using My Senses

©2005 by Evan-Moor Corp.
All About My World • EMC 2403

Using My Senses

©2005 by Evan-Moor Corp.
All About My World • EMC 2403

Using My Senses

©2005 by Evan-Moor Corp.
All About My World • EMC 2403

Using My Senses

©2005 by Evan-Moor Corp.
All About My World • EMC 2403

Using My Senses

©2005 by Evan-Moor Corp.
All About My World • EMC 2403

Using My Senses

©2005 by Evan-Moor Corp.
All About My World • EMC 2403

Using My Senses

©2005 by Evan-Moor Corp.
All About My World • EMC 2403

Using My Senses

©2005 by Evan-Moor Corp.
All About My World • EMC 2403

Using My Senses

©2005 by Evan-Moor Corp.
All About My World • EMC 2403

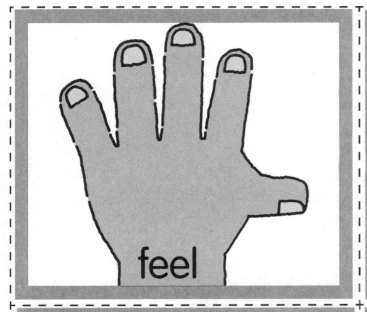

feel

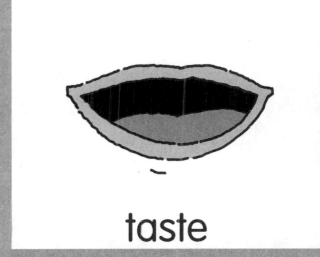

taste

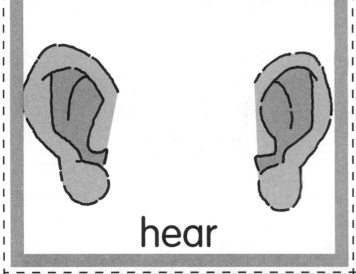

hear

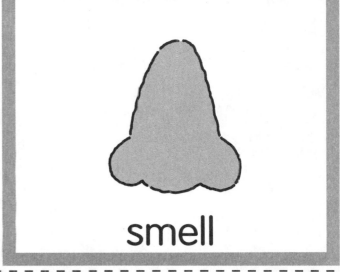

smell

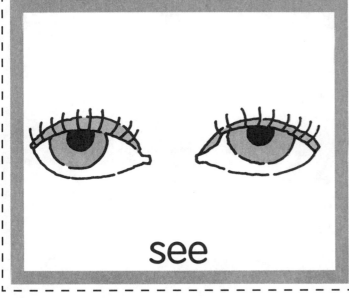

see

Using My Senses

Using My Senses

©2005 by Evan-Moor Corp.
All About My World • EMC 2403

Using My Senses

©2005 by Evan-Moor Corp.
All About My World • EMC 2403

Using My Senses

©2005 by Evan-Moor Corp.
All About My World • EMC 2403

Using My Senses

©2005 by Evan-Moor Corp.
All About My World • EMC 2403

Using My Senses

©2005 by Evan-Moor Corp.
All About My World • EMC 2403

Using My Senses

©2005 by Evan-Moor Corp.
All About My World • EMC 2403

Children take turns leading the class in simple physical exercises.

Materials

- page 48, reproduced
- paper bag

Exercise Makes a Healthy Me

Preparation

1. Reproduce page 48 two times. Cut out the exercise pictures. You may wish to laminate them for durability.
2. Place the pictures in a paper bag.
3. Plan to play in an outdoor area.

How to Play

1. Select a child to choose an exercise card from the paper bag. Allow the child to decide how many times the class will perform the exercise.
2. Model the exercise for the class.
3. Allow the child to lead the class in performing the exercise.
4. Continue to play until each child has had an opportunity to be the leader.

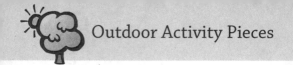

Outdoor Activity Pieces

Note: Reproduce this page to use with Exercise Makes a Healthy Me outdoor activity.

stretch

hop

touch toes

jump

arm circles

twist

skip

reach for feet

bend

Note: Sing this song to the tune of "If You're Happy and You Know It."

Music/Dramatic Play Activity

A familiar tune, new words, and movement provide a musical way for children to learn about their bodies.

Sing-Along Body Song

If you're happy and you know it, raise your arms.
If you're happy and you know it, raise your arms.
If you're happy and you know it,
Find that body part and show it!
If you're happy and you know it, raise your arms.

If you're happy and you know it, stomp your feet.
If you're happy and you know it, stomp your feet.
If you're happy and you know it,
Find that body part and show it!
If you're happy and you know it, stomp your feet.

If you're happy and you know it, clap your hands.
If you're happy and you know it, clap your hands.
If you're happy and you know it,
Find that body part and show it!
If you're happy and you know it, clap your hands.

Other action choices:

- blink your eyes
- wiggle your hips
- tap your toes
- point your finger
- shrug your shoulders
- touch your elbows
- bend your knees

- nod your head
- jump up high
- snap your fingers
- reach down low
- stand on tiptoes
- wiggle your nose
- touch your ears

All About My Family

Children learn the names of different family members and about activities that families do together.

Families
Are Special

Hello, my name is Jimmy.
I'd like you to meet my family.
Families are special.

This is my father.
He helps me feel better
when I'm feeling sad.

2

This is my mother.
She tucks me in bed and whispers,
"Good night."

This is my sister.
She helps me cross
the street safely.

This is my brother.
We like to play games together.

This is my grandma.
We like to draw together.

Families are special.
Tell me about your family!

The End

Families Are Special

Hello, my name is Jimmy. I'd like you to meet my family. Families are special.

1

This is my father.
He helps me feel better
when I'm feeling sad.

2

This is my mother.
She tucks me in bed and
whispers, "Good night."

3

This is my sister.
She helps me cross
the street safely.

4

This is my brother.
We like to play
games together.

5

This is my grandma.
We like to draw together.

6

This is my grandpa.
We like to take walks
and talk.

7

Families are special.

Tell me about your family!

8

The End

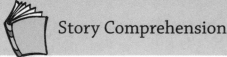
Note: Children color *yes* if the picture is from the story Families Are Special and *no* if it is not.

Name _____

Families Are Special

Was it in the story? ☺ yes
                          ☹ no

Note: See page 7 for suggestions on using the storyboard pieces on pages 67 and 69 for Families Are Special.

Storyboard Pieces

All About
My Family

All About
My Family

All About
My Family

All About
My Family

mother	Jimmy
father	sister
grandma	brother
grandpa	pet

**All About
My Family**

©2005 by Evan-Moor Corp.
All About My World
EMC 2403

**All About
My Family**

©2005 by Evan-Moor Corp.
All About My World
EMC 2403

**All About
My Family**

©2005 by Evan-Moor Corp.
All About My World
EMC 2403

All About My Family

©2005 by Evan-Moor Corp.
All About My World
EMC 2403

All About My Family

©2005 by Evan-Moor Corp.
All About My World
EMC 2403

All About My Family

©2005 by Evan-Moor Corp.
All About My World
EMC 2403

All About My Family

©2005 by Evan-Moor Corp.
All About My World
EMC 2403

All About My Family

©2005 by Evan-Moor Corp.
All About My World
EMC 2403

All About My Family

©2005 by Evan-Moor Corp.
All About My World
EMC 2403

**All About
My Family**

©2005 by
Evan-Moor Corp.
All About My World
EMC 2403

All About My Family

©2005 by Evan-Moor Corp.
All About My World
EMC 2403

Children decorate cutouts of themselves and family members.

Materials

- page 72, reproduced
- 12" x 18" (30.5 x 45.5 cm) white construction paper, one sheet per child
- scissors, crayons, and glue
- paper scraps in a variety of colors
- brown, yellow, and black yarn

Meet My Family

Preparation

1. Ask children how many members are in their immediate family. Use the result of your poll to calculate how many times you will need to reproduce page 72. Reproduce page 72 on a variety of skin-toned construction paper.

2. Plan time to model the steps for this project and a completed Meet My Family picture.

Steps to Follow

1. Children cut out the correct number and size of people figures to represent their family.

2. They color and decorate the figures to resemble family members.

3. Children glue the family member figures on the construction paper.

4. They write each family member's name above that person's picture.

Art Activity Pattern Pieces

Note: Reproduce these patterns to use with Meet My Family art activity.

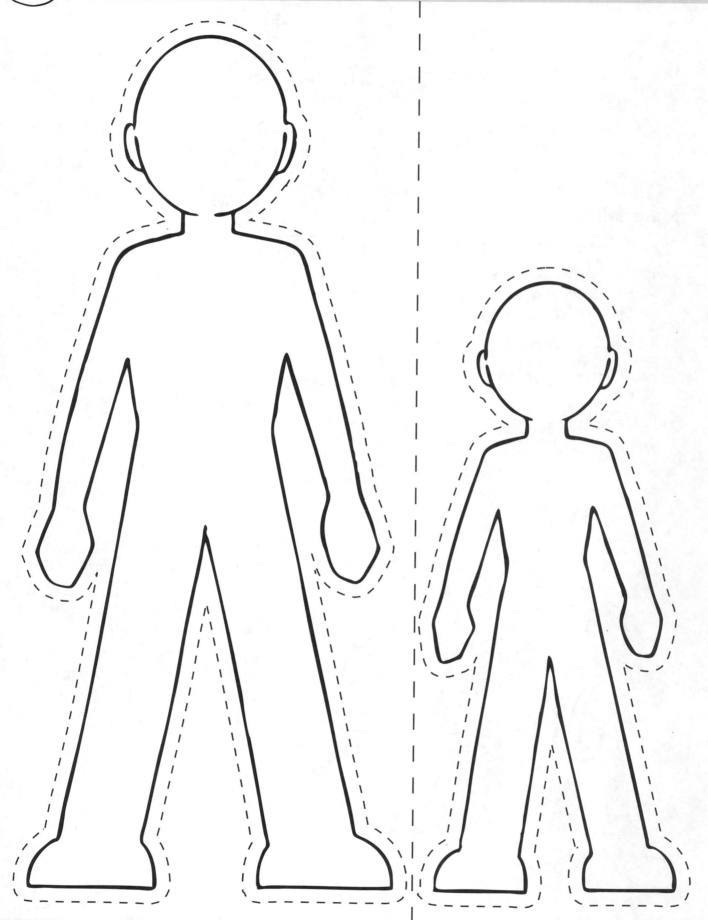

Note: Check for allergies before beginning any cooking activity.
An allergic reaction can occur through taste, smell, or contact with allergens.

Cooking Activity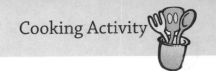

Family-Style Vegetable Soup

Materials

- stove or hot plate for cooking soup
- large stockpot with lid
- large spoon or soup ladle
- can opener
- knife (adult use only)
- 6 cups of water
- 2 large cans of tomato juice
- 6 chicken or beef bouillon cubes
- a variety of canned, frozen, or fresh vegetables, such as corn, green beans, yellow beans, peas, lima beans, carrots, potatoes, celery, cabbage, onions, lentils, and tomatoes
- paper soup bowls
- plastic spoons
- soup crackers

Preparation

1. Explain to children that vegetables contain vitamins that people need to stay healthy. Tell children they will make soup using different vegetables.
2. Ask each child to bring a vegetable to add to the soup.
3. Plan time to discuss the steps for making vegetable soup.

Steps to Follow

1. Children measure 6 cups of water and pour it into the stockpot. Children pour two cans of tomato juice into the stockpot.
2. Then they count and add the bouillon cubes to the stockpot.
3. Children add vegetables to the soup mixture in the stockpot.
4. Then they stir the soup as each ingredient is added.
5. Once all the ingredients have been added, place the stockpot on a stove burner or hot plate. Cook on low heat, stirring periodically, for about one hour.
6. Once the soup is finished cooking and is sufficiently cool, ladle it into the paper bowls.
7. Serve with soup crackers and enjoy!

Dear Parent(s) or Guardian(s),

Today we cooked in class. Your child helped prepare "Family-Style Vegetable Soup." Besides having fun cooking and eating, the children practiced these skills:

- counting
- measurement
- vocabulary development

For our unit *My World*, we will send home a variety of new recipes. Each recipe will be one that your child has tried in class and is excited about. We hope you have an opportunity to try this recipe again with your child. Allowing your child to help you in the kitchen is a wonderful way to reinforce learning skills while creating family memories.

Family-Style Vegetable Soup

Materials

- large stockpot with lid
- large spoon for stirring
- soup ladle for serving
- can opener
- knife (adult use only)
- 6 chicken or beef bouillon cubes
- 6 cups of water
- 2 large cans of tomato juice
- a variety of canned, frozen, or fresh vegetables, such as corn, green beans, yellow beans, peas, lima beans, carrots, potatoes, celery, cabbage, onions, lentils, and tomatoes
- paper soup bowls
- plastic spoons
- soup crackers

Steps to Follow

1. Place the bouillon cubes, water, and tomato juice in a large stockpot.

2. Gradually add a variety of your family's favorite vegetables to the soup broth and stir.

3. Cover pot with a lid and cook slowly for about 1 hour until all vegetables are cooked or heated through. Stir soup as it cooks.

4. Once the soup is finished cooking and is sufficiently cool, ladle it into the paper bowls.

5. Serve with soup crackers and enjoy!

Note: Children say the names of the pictures in each row and color the picture that rhymes with the first picture in each row.

Language—Auditory Discrimination ABC

Name _____

Bat Sounds Like Cat

Color the picture that rhymes with the first picture in each row.

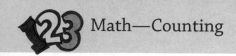

Note: Children count each set of objects and draw a line to the correct numeral.

Name _____

Counting Is Fun!

Count. Draw a line.

 - - - - - - - - - - - - - - - - - - **2**

 **7**

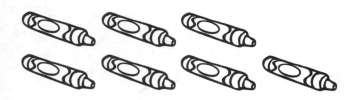 **10**

 **4**

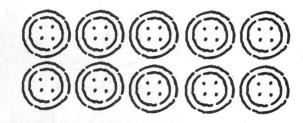 **5**

Note: Children cut and glue the pictures below to complete each pattern.

Name _____

Finish the Pattern

Cut.  Glue.

			glue	glue
			glue	glue
		glue	glue	

All About My Family   **77**

Children match sets of twins, each with an identical outfit.

Materials

- pages 79 and 81
- sturdy folder or envelope

Twins in the Family

Creating the Center

1. Laminate and cut out pages 79 and 81.

2. Store the cards in a sturdy folder or envelope. Label the folder or envelope.

3. Explain to children that sometimes families have twins. Point out that twins sometimes like to dress alike.

4. Plan time to model how the center is used.

Using the Center

1. Children match the twin cards correctly.

2. Then they mix the cards up and turn them facedown.

3. Children play a game of memory with the cards.

Twins in the Family

Twins in the Family

Twins in the Family

Twins in the Family

Twins in the Family

Twins in the Family

Twins in the Family

©2005 by Evan-Moor Corp.
All About My World • EMC 2403

Twins in the Family

©2005 by Evan-Moor Corp.
All About My World • EMC 2403

Twins in the Family

©2005 by Evan-Moor Corp.
All About My World • EMC 2403

Twins in the Family

©2005 by Evan-Moor Corp.
All About My World • EMC 2403

Twins in the Family

©2005 by Evan-Moor Corp.
All About My World • EMC 2403

Twins in the Family

©2005 by Evan-Moor Corp.
All About My World • EMC 2403

Note: Demonstrate and practice the game steps before beginning the game.

Outdoor Activity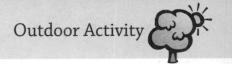

Children listen to directions in order to be the first to reach "Mother."

Kinds of Game Steps

- **Giant step** (large, striding steps)

- **Baby step** (small, halting steps)

- **Hopping step** (jumping up and forward with two feet)

- **Leaping step** (bounding forward with one foot and landing on two feet)

- **Tiptoe step** (walking in small steps, up on toes)

- **Twirling/ballerina step** (twirling in small circles while advancing forward)

- **Galloping step** (trotting like a horse)

- **Backward step** (walking backward)

Mother May I...?

Preparation

1. Explain to children that the object of the game is to be the first person to reach Mother. Tell them that they can accomplish this by listening closely to Mother's directions.

2. Plan to play in an outdoor space.

How to Play

1. Divide the class into four groups. Have each group line up at opposite ends of the play yard, all of them facing Mother (the teacher).

2. Explain to children that they must always ask *Mother may I?*, and listen for *Yes you may*, before they take any steps toward Mother. Tell children that if they forget to ask *Mother may I?* before they move, they must stay in place and wait for their next turn.

3. Mother stands in the middle of the groups and says,

   Teacher: *Group 1, you may take three giant steps.*

   Group 1: *Mother may I?*

   Teacher: responds, *Yes you may* or, *No you may not.*

   Teacher repeats the same type and number of steps to Groups 2, 3, and 4.

4. The first group or person to reach Mother wins.

 Music/Dramatic Play Activity

Note: Teach this song to the tune of "You Are My Sunshine."

You Are My Family

You are my family
My special family
You take care of me
Every day.
It's so much fun when
We're together
We love to sing, to laugh,
and to play.

You are my family
My special family
We help each other
In every way.
When Mom is cooking
Dad is cleaning
I like to help them every day.

—Lisa Mathews

Playing House

Children pretend to be different members of their family.

Preparation

1. Set up a dramatic play center that includes props such as: grown-up clothes, hats, a briefcase, a laundry basket, school books, a pretend oven/stove, and kitchenware.

2. Allow children to share their perceptions of what their family members do at work, home, and school.

3. Explain to children that they will go to the dramatic play center and pretend to be different members of their family.

How to Play

1. Children "dress up" like the person they are pretending to be.

2. Children pretend to perform household duties, work duties, and school duties using the props from the dramatic play center.

All About My Friends

Children learn that friends are people with whom
they laugh, play, eat, share, talk, and take turns.

My Friends

When I went to school, I felt all alone.

Then I met Jose, Mei Lin, and Tyrone.

We laughed and we played.
Then we sat down to eat.

Some of us liked pizza.
Some of us liked meat.

We are all friends.
We help and we share.

We talk and we listen.
We take turns because we care.

My friends and I sing and dance together.

We hope to be friends forever and ever!

8

The End

My Friends

When I went to school,
I felt all alone.

1

Then I met Jose,

Mei Lin, and Tyrone.

2

We laughed and we played.

Then we sat down to eat.

3

Some of us liked pizza.

Some of us liked meat.

4

We are all friends.

We help and we share.

5

We talk and we listen.
We take turns because
we care.

6

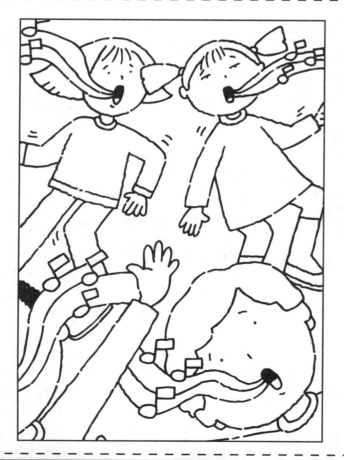

My friends and I sing
and dance together.

7

We hope to be friends forever and ever!

8

The End

Note: Children color and cut out the pictures and place them in the order in which they appeared in My Friends.

Name _____

1, 2, 3

Color. Cut. ✂ Glue. 🖊

glue	glue	glue
1	**2**	**3**

Note: See page 8 for suggestions on using the storyboard pieces on pages 103 and 105 for My Friends.

All About
My Friends

All About
My Friends

All About
My Friends

All About
My Friends

All About My Friends

All About
My Friends

All About
My Friends

All About
My Friends

All About
My Friends

All About
My Friends

Children enjoy running across the grass and watching the butterflies and airplanes "fly" in the breeze.

Friendly Flyers

Preparation

1. Prepare an art center with all materials assembled.

2. Allow children to choose which Friendly Flyer they would like to make. Based upon their choices, reproduce pages 108 and 109 on white construction paper.

3. Cut the yarn into pieces and tie a loop at one end of each piece.

Materials

- pages 108 and 109, reproduced
- 8 ½" x 11" (21.5 x 28 cm) white construction paper, one sheet per child
- yarn
- scissors
- glue
- crayons or markers
- hole punch

Steps to Follow

1. Children decorate their pattern.

2. They fold the pattern and cut on the dotted line.

3. They glue the 2 parts together.

4. Children punch the hole where marked and pull the yarn through. Help the children tie a knot.

5. They go outside to play with their friendly flyers.

Extension

Hang the friendly flyers from the ceiling or near a window or doorway to fly in the breeze.

Friendly
Flyer

fold

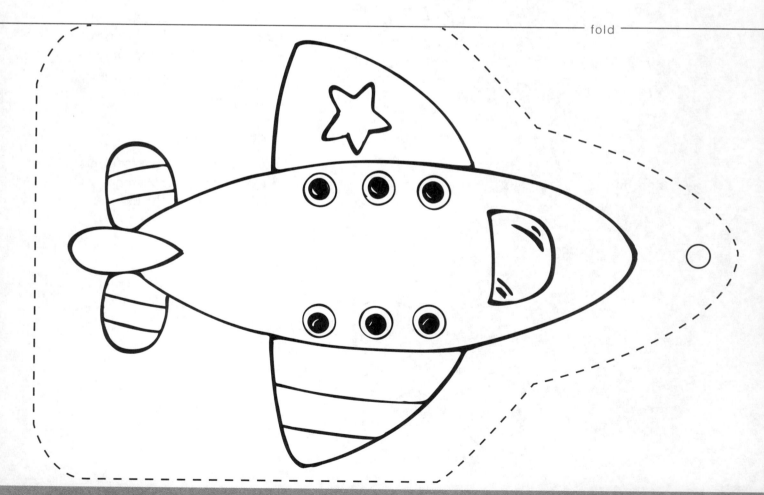

Friendly
Flyer

fold ——————————————————————————— fold

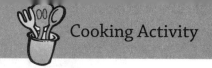
Note: Check for allergies before beginning any cooking activity. An allergic reaction can occur through taste, smell, or contact with allergens.

Friendship Bracelets

Children create two friendship bracelets, one for themselves and one for a friend.

Preparation

1. Cut two pieces of string licorice for each child. Tie a knot at the end of each piece. (Be sure to cut pieces long enough to circle a child's wrist and tie together.)

2. Review the concept of patterning with children.

3. Model a completed Friendship Bracelet. Explain the pattern you used to create the bracelet.

4. Explain to children that they will make one friendship bracelet for themselves and one for a friend.

Materials

- string licorice, two pieces per child

- donut-shaped colored cereal pieces

Steps to Follow

1. Children choose cereal pieces and lay them out in a pattern.

2. Children thread the licorice through the cereal pieces.

3. Once children have completed a bracelet, they ask a teacher to tie the ends together.

4. Children follow the steps above to make a second bracelet.

5. Children have a friendship bracelet exchange and a yummy snack!

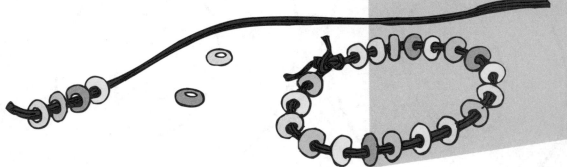

All About My World • EMC 2403 • ©2005 by Evan-Moor Corp.

Dear Parent(s) or Guardian(s),

Today we cooked in class. Your child made "Friendship Bracelets." Besides having fun cooking and eating, the children practiced these skills:

- listening to and following directions
- patterning
- using small motor skills

For our unit *My World*, we will send home a variety of new recipes. Each recipe will be one that your child has tried in class and is excited about. We hope you have an opportunity to try this recipe again with your child. Allowing your child to help you in the kitchen is a wonderful way to reinforce learning skills while creating family memories.

Friendship Bracelets

Materials

- string licorice, long enough to circle a wrist and tie
- donut-shaped colored cereal pieces

Steps to Follow

1. Tie one end of the licorice so that the cereal doesn't slide off.
2. Thread the colored cereal onto the licorice, creating a pattern.
3. Once the bracelet is completed, tie the ends together.
4. Have a family friendship bracelet exchange.

Note: Children color the picture in each row that is different.

Name _____

Same or Different?

Color the picture in each row that is different.

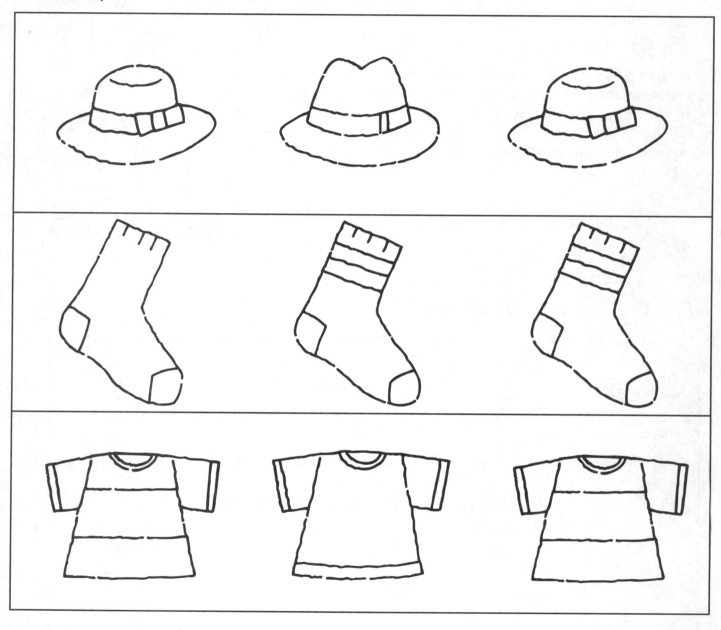

Count how many.

 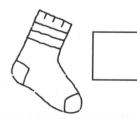 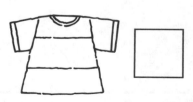

Note: Children say the name of each picture aloud. Children color the pictures that begin with the letter *h*.

Language—Letter and Sound Recognition

Name _____

It Starts with Hh

hat

Color the pictures that begin with **h**.

Note: Assist children in completing the color key below. Children follow the key to color the pictures.

Name _____

Color the Shapes

Color. 🖍

yellow   purple   orange   red

All About My World • EMC 2403 • ©2005 by Evan-Moor Corp.

Note: Children add the hats and write the sum in the box.

Name _____

How Many Hats?

 + =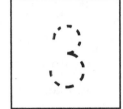

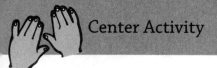

What Are They Playing?

Children match friend task cards with sports equipment task cards.

Creating the Center

1. Laminate and cut out pages 117 and 119.

2. Place the friend task cards in an envelope. Label it. Place the sports equipment task cards in another envelope. Label it.

3. Store envelopes in a sturdy folder or larger envelope.

4. Plan time to model how the center is used.

Using the Center

1. Children match the two friends that are playing the same sport.

2. Then they match the friend task cards with the correct sports equipment task card.

3. Children self-check their matches by turning the friend task cards over and matching the word on the backside to the word on the sports task card.

Materials

- pages 117 and 119

- scissors

- 2 envelopes

- sturdy folder or envelope

All About My Friends

soccer

soccer

baseball

baseball

football

football

basketball

basketball

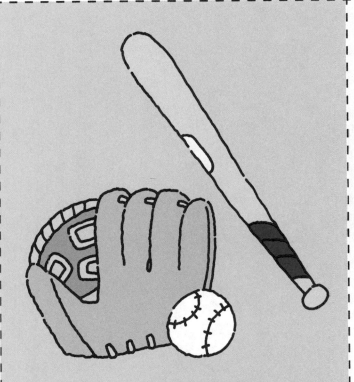

baseball

soccer

football

basketball

What Are They Playing?

What Are They Playing?

What Are They Playing?

What Are They Playing?

Watch Us Move

Partners sing a chant to demonstrate an action for the whole class to follow.

Preparation

1. Divide the children into sets of two.

2. Model different ways to move (for example, walking, running, jumping with two feet, jumping with one foot, leaping, galloping, skipping, sliding front/back, spinning, and hopping).

3. Explain to children that each pair of partners will lead the class in a different way to move their bodies.

4. Plan to play in an outdoor space.

How to Play

1. Pairs of partners face each other with 10–15 feet between them. Partners decide which action they will demonstrate in front of the class.

2. One pair of children stands in front of the class and demonstrates an action for the whole class to follow.

3. The rest of the pairs face each other and follow the action being demonstrated.

4. Each pair of partners takes a turn demonstrating an action in front of the class.

5. The activity continues until all the partners have had a turn leading the class.

Note: Sing this song to the tune of "London Bridge."

Friends Sing-Along

My friends and I like to play,
Like to play,
Like to play.
My friends and I like to play,
Play all day.

We like to sing and dance,
Sing and dance,
Sing and dance.
We like to sing and dance,
All day long.

Friends are fun to have,
Fun to have,
Fun to have.
Friends are fun to have.
Friends are fun!

Reproduce page 123 for children to draw a picture of themselves and a friend doing their favorite activity.

Me and My Friend

All About My Home

Children learn about rooms
in a house and activities
that commonly occur there.

Hide-and-Seek

Let's all play hide-and-seek.
Close your eyes—then take a peek.

Can you find me? Look all around.
Look right and left—then up and down.

Am I in the kitchen, hiding by the sink?
Take a look. What do you think?

Am I in the bedroom,
hiding under the bed?
No, it's just my dog—that sleepyhead!

Am I in the bathroom, hiding in the tub—
Where I scrub with a rub-a-dub-dub?

Am I in the living room, hiding near the chairs—in the closet or around the stairs?

Am I hiding down the hall?
There are no more rooms.
You have searched them all!

Here I am. You have finally found me.
Oh! What fun hide-and-seek can be!

The End

Note: Teachers will make copies and cut in half for minibooks.

Reproducible Story

Hide-and-Seek

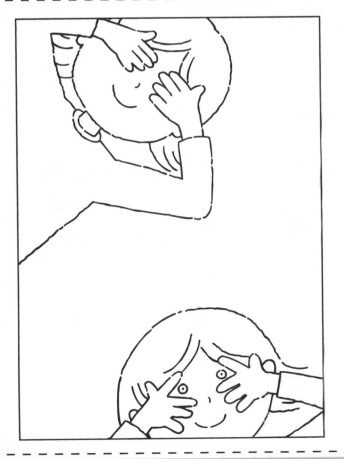

Let's all play hide-and-seek.
Close your eyes—then take
a peek.

1

Can you find me?
Look all around.
Look right and
left—then up
and down.

2

Am I in the kitchen,
hiding by the sink?
Take a look. What
do you think?

3

Am I in the bedroom,
hiding under the bed?
No, it's just my dog—
that sleepyhead!

4

Am I in the bathroom,
hiding in the tub—
Where I scrub with
a rub-a-dub-dub?

5

Am I in the living room,
hiding near the chairs—
in the closet or around
the stairs?

6

Am I hiding down
the hall?
There are no more
rooms. You have
searched them all!

7

Here I am. You have finally found me. Oh! What fun hide-and-seek can be!

8

The End

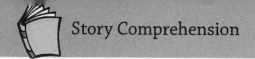

Name _____

Where Does It Belong?

Draw a line.

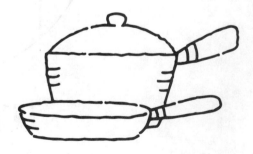

Note: See page 8 for suggestions on using the storyboard pieces on pages 141 and 143 for Hide-and-Seek.

Storyboard Pieces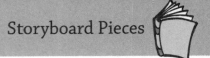

All About My Home

All About My Home

All About My Home

All About My Home

All About My Home

All About My Home

hallway	living room
kitchen	bathroom
bedroom	toothpaste
pillow	pots

All About My Home

©2005 by Evan-Moor Corp.
All About My World • EMC 2403

All About My Home

©2005 by Evan-Moor Corp.
All About My World • EMC 2403

All About My Home

©2005 by Evan-Moor Corp.
All About My World • EMC 2403

All About My Home

©2005 by Evan-Moor Corp.
All About My World • EMC 2403

All About My Home

©2005 by Evan-Moor Corp.
All About My World • EMC 2403

All About My Home

©2005 by Evan-Moor Corp.
All About My World • EMC 2403

All About My Home

©2005 by Evan-Moor Corp.
All About My World • EMC 2403

All About My Home

©2005 by Evan-Moor Corp.
All About My World • EMC 2403

All About My Home

©2005 by Evan-Moor Corp.
All About My World • EMC 2403

Children paint colorful pictures of their favorite room in their house.

Materials

- large paint paper
- tempera paint in various colors
- paint brushes
- paint smocks or aprons

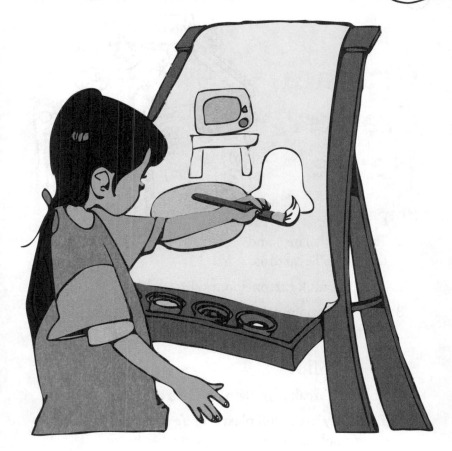

Just Picture My House!

Preparation

1. Prepare a painting area with all materials assembled.
2. Review objects that are typically found in different rooms of a house.

Steps to Follow

1. Children think about their favorite room in their house.
2. They paint a picture of their favorite room in their house.
3. Once children finish painting their favorite room, they tell the class about what they painted and why the room is their favorite.

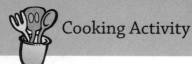
Note: Check for allergies before beginning any cooking activity. An allergic reaction can occur through taste, smell, or contact with allergens.

Graham Cracker House

Preparation

1. Thoroughly rinse and dry the milk cartons.

2. Tape the milk carton spouts closed.

3. Plan time to model the steps for this project and a completed Graham Cracker House.

Steps to Follow

1. Children break 3 graham crackers in half.

2. Then they use a dull plastic knife to spread frosting on one side of the six graham cracker halves.

3. Children press one graham cracker half to each side of the carton, and two graham cracker halves to the top of the milk carton.

4. Then they decorate their graham cracker house by using vanilla frosting to adhere small candies to the graham crackers.

5. Once children finish their graham cracker houses, allow them to display the houses on their desks for a class-wide "open house."

Children create tasty graham cracker houses out of milk cartons.

Materials

- empty half-pint-sized milk cartons, 1 per child

- graham crackers, 3 per child

- vanilla frosting

- dull plastic knives

- masking tape

- small candies

  M&M's®

  miniature marshmallows

  small pretzels

  colorful cereal

  Lifesaver® candies

  candy jimmies

  chocolate chips

Dear Parent(s) or Guardian(s),

Today we cooked in class. Your child made a "Graham Cracker House." Besides having fun cooking and eating, the children practiced these skills:

- listening to and following directions
- using small motor skills
- vocabulary and concept development

For our unit *My World*, we will send home a variety of new recipes. Each recipe will be one that your child has tried in class and is excited about. We hope you have an opportunity to try this recipe again with your child. Allowing your child to help you in the kitchen is a wonderful way to reinforce learning skills while creating family memories.

Graham Cracker House

Materials

- empty half-pint-size milk carton
- graham crackers, 3 per house
- vanilla frosting
- dull plastic knife
- masking tape
- small candies
  - M&M's®
  - miniature marshmallows
  - small pretzels
  - colorful cereal
  - Lifesaver® candies
  - candy jimmies
  - chocolate chips

Steps to Follow

1. Wash and dry an empty half-pint-size milk carton.
2. Tape the spout closed.
3. Break 3 graham crackers in half. Use a dull plastic knife to spread frosting on one side of the six graham cracker halves.
4. Press one graham cracker half to each side of the carton, and two graham cracker halves to the top of the milk carton.
5. Decorate the graham cracker house by using vanilla frosting to adhere small candies to the graham crackers.
6. Enjoy!

Note: Children say the name of the picture at the beginning of each row and listen to the beginning sound. Children color the picture that has the same beginning sound as the first picture in each row.

Name _____

They Start the Same

Color the picture that has the same beginning sound as the first picture in each row.

All About My World • EMC 2403 • ©2005 by Evan-Moor Corp.

Note: Review color words with children. You may wish to display a chart with the colors and their names as a guide for young learners. Review the names of the geometric shapes. Lead children in coloring the key below.

Name _____

Color the Shapes

Color 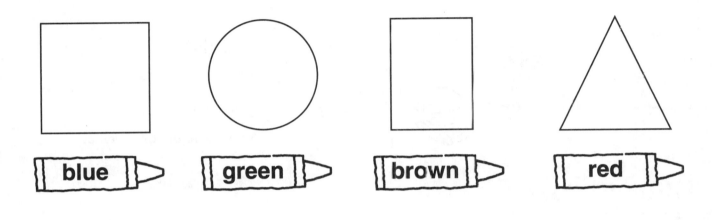 the shapes.

| blue | green | brown | red |

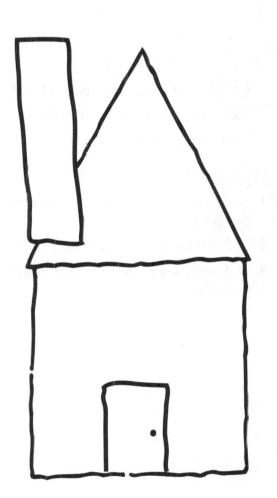

Children place various household objects in their proper place.

Materials

- pages 151 and 153
- scissors
- sturdy folder or envelope

Everything Has a Place

Creating the Center

1. Laminate and cut out pages 151 and 153.
2. Store the cards in a sturdy folder or envelope.
3. Plan time to model how the center is used.

Using the Center

1. Children sort the household item task cards into groups.
2. Children lay the furniture task cards out.
3. Children place each household item task card in its proper place.

**Everything Has
a Place**

©2005 by Evan-Moor Corp.
All About My World • EMC 2403

Everything Has a Place

©2005 by Evan-Moor Corp.
All About My World • EMC 2403

**Everything Has
a Place**

©2005 by Evan-Moor Corp.
All About My World • EMC 2403

**Everything Has
a Place**

©2005 by Evan-Moor Corp.
All About My World • EMC 2403

**Everything Has
a Place**

©2005 by Evan-Moor Corp.
All About My World • EMC 2403

**Everything Has
a Place**

©2005 by Evan-Moor Corp.
All About My World • EMC 2403

**Everything Has
a Place**

©2005 by Evan-Moor Corp.
All About My World • EMC 2403

**Everything Has
a Place**

©2005 by Evan-Moor Corp.
All About My World • EMC 2403

Everything Has a Place

©2005 by Evan-Moor Corp.
All About My World • EMC 2403

**Everything Has
a Place**

©2005 by Evan-Moor Corp.
All About My World • EMC 2403

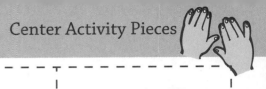

All About My Home   **153**

Everything Has
a Place

Everything Has
a Place

Everything Has a Place

Everything Has
a Place

Everything Has
a Place

Everything Has
a Place

Everything Has a Place

Everything Has
a Place

In this fun game children run away when they hear "It's bedtime!"

What Time Is It?

Preparation

1. Explain to children that the object of this game is to avoid getting caught for bedtime.

2. Tell children that the number of steps they move forward must correspond with the number in the time you have said. For example, if you say the time is 4 o'clock, then children take four steps forward.

3. Plan to play in an outdoor space.

How to Play

1. Children line up shoulder to shoulder.

2. The teacher stands in front of the class and says, *Your bedtime is _____ o'clock.*

3. The teacher turns her back and waits for the children to call out, *What time is it?*

4. The teacher turns around and answers, *It's _____ o'clock!*

5. Children take the corresponding number of steps forward. If the teacher answers, *It's 9 o'clock! It's bedtime!* the children immediately run back to the start line before the teacher can catch them.

6. Play again as time allows. Change the "bedtime" each time you play.

This Is the Way I...

Preparation

1. Reproduce page 157 for each child.

2. Familiarize yourself with the tune of the song "This Is the Way We...."

Steps to Follow

1. Explain to children that they will be singing a movement song.

2. Sing and demonstrate the first verse of the song. Invite children to sing the verse with you and make up accompanying movements.

3. Sing and demonstrate the other three verses.

4. Have children practice singing and performing the movements for the verses.

5. Suggestions for additional verses could include: kitchen—set the table, cook the food; living room—watch TV, play a game; bathroom—wash myself, comb my hair, floss my teeth; and, bedroom—turn off the light, say my prayers, snuggle my stuffed animal, etc.

Children sing and perform movements while learning about activities that occur in various rooms of a house.

This Is the Way I...

This is the way I brush my teeth
Brush my teeth
Brush my teeth
This is the way I brush my teeth
In the bathroom in my house.

This is the way I sleep all night
Sleep all night
Sleep all night
This is the way I sleep all night
In the bedroom in my house.

This is the way I wash the dishes
Wash the dishes
Wash the dishes
This is the way I wash the dishes
In the kitchen in my house.

This is the way I read a book
Read a book
Read a book
This is the way I read a book
In the living room in my house.

5

All About My Neighborhood

Children learn that neighborhoods
consist of a variety of people, jobs, and places.

My Neighborhood

I walk down a street in my neighborhood.
My neighbor Mr. Friendly asks me,
"Are you going to school today?"
"Not today," I answer.

I walk down a street in my neighborhood.
The mail carrier asks me,
"Do you have cards to mail today?"
"Not today," I answer.

I walk down a street in my neighborhood.
I see the fire station and the police station.

The police officers are checking bicycles.
Officer Tom asks me,
"Do you want your bike checked today?"
"Not today," I answer.

I walk down a street in my neighborhood.
I see the pet store, the bookstore,
and the grocery store. Mr. Ed asks me,
"Do you want an apple today?"
"Not today," I answer.

I walk down a street in my neighborhood.
I see my doctor's office. Doctor Sue asks me,
"Do you need to see me today?"
"Not today," I answer.

I walk down a street in my neighborhood.
I see the library, the school, and the playground.

My friend is at the playground.
He asks me, "Do you have time to play?"
"Yes, today I can play," I answer.

The End

Note: teachers will make copies and cut in half for minibooks.

Reproducible Story

My Neighborhood

I walk down a street
in my neighborhood.
My neighbor Mr. Friendly
asks me, "Are you
going to school today?"

"Not today," I answer.

1

I walk down a street in
my neighborhood.
The mail carrier asks me,
"Do you have cards to
mail today?"

"Not today," I answer.

2

I walk down a street in
my neighborhood.
I see the fire station and
the police station.

3

All About My Neighborhood
All About My World • EMC 2403 • ©2005 by Evan-Moor Corp.

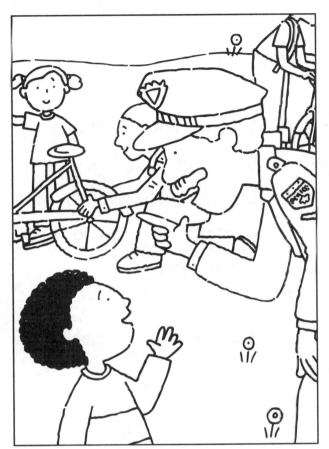

The police officers are checking bicycles. Officer Tom asks me, "Do you want your bike checked today?"

"Not today." I answer.

4

I walk down a street in my neighborhood. I see the pet store, the bookstore, and the grocery store. Mr. Ed asks me, "Do you want an apple today?"

"Not today," I answer.

5

I walk down a street in my neighborhood. I see my doctor's office. Doctor Sue asks me, "Do you need to see me today?"

"Not today," I answer.

6

I walk down a street in my neighborhood. I see the library, the school, and the playground.

7

My friend is at
the playground.
He asks me,
"Do you have
time to play?"

"Yes, today I can play,"
I answer.

8

The End

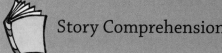
Note: Children color the people from My Neighborhood circle-time story.

Name _____

People from My Neighborhood

Color the people from the story.

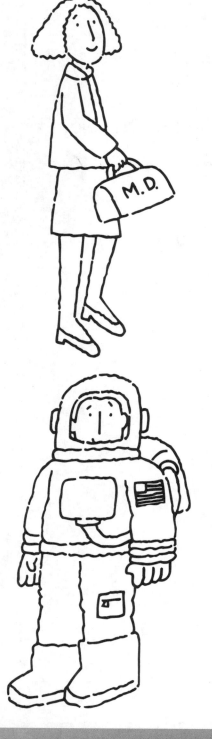

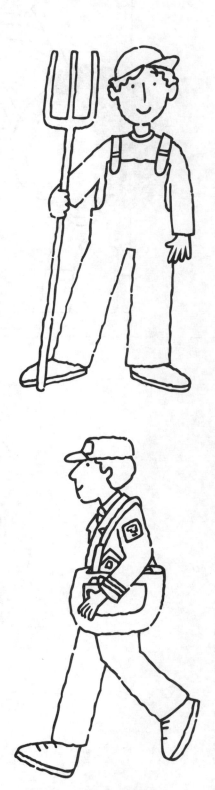

Note: See page 9 for suggestions on using the storyboard pieces on pages 175 and 177 for My Neighborhood.

Storyboard Pieces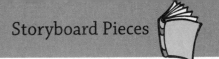

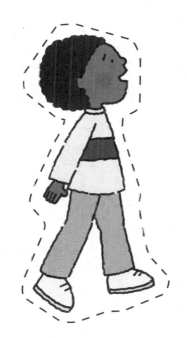

policeman

mail carrier

All About My
Neighborhood

©2005 by Evan-Moor Corp.
All About My World • EMC 2403

All About My Neighborhood

©2005 by Evan-Moor Corp.
All About My World • EMC 2403

All About My
Neighborhood

©2005 by Evan-Moor Corp.
All About My World • EMC 2403

All About My
Neighborhood

©2005 by Evan-Moor Corp.
All About My World • EMC 2403

All About My Neighborhood

©2005 by Evan-Moor Corp.
All About My World • EMC 2403

All About My Neighborhood

©2005 by Evan-Moor Corp.
All About My World • EMC 2403

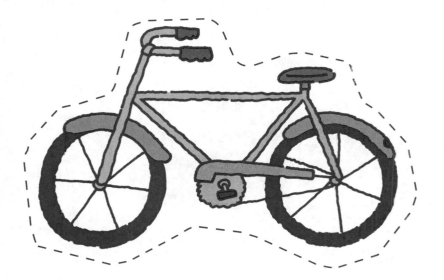

Doctor's Office Building

Dr. Sue...........................1A

doctor | friends

**All About My
Neighborhood**

©2005 by Evan-Moor Corp.
All About My World • EMC 2403

**All About My
Neighborhood**

©2005 by Evan-Moor Corp.
All About My World • EMC 2403

**All About My
Neighborhood**

©2005 by Evan-Moor Corp.
All About My World • EMC 2403

**All About My
Neighborhood**

©2005 by Evan-Moor Corp.
All About My World • EMC 2403

**All About My
Neighborhood**

©2005 by Evan-Moor Corp.
All About My World • EMC 2403

**All About My
Neighborhood**

©2005 by Evan-Moor Corp.
All About My World • EMC 2403

Create a Neighborhood

Preparation

1. Prepare an art center with all materials assembled.
2. Cut 12" x 18" (30.5 x 45.5 cm) construction paper in half lengthwise. Each child will use one half of the paper for this project.
3. Reproduce page 180 for each child.
4. Reproduce page 181 for each child.

Steps to Follow

1. Children take one half of the 12" x 18" (30.5 x 45.5 cm) construction paper and fold the paper in an accordion style, making 4 sections.

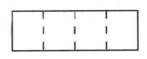

2. Children color and cut out the 4 sections on page 180. Glue one section to each part of the construction paper.
3. Children display their neighborhood on their desk. They cut out the children on page 181 and fold on the fold line. The children can then be placed in front of each of the neighborhood buildings.

Children fold, cut, and glue to create a neighborhood.

Materials

- pages 180 and 181, reproduced
- 12" x 18" (30.5 x 45.5 cm) construction paper
- scissors
- glue
- colored pencils

Art Activity Pattern Pieces

Note: Reproduce these patterns to use with Create a Neighborhood art activity.

Pet Store

OPEN

Library

ENTER

Bakery

OPEN

My Neighborhood

name

Note: Reprocuce these patterns to use
with Create a Neighborhood art activity.

Art Activity Pattern Pieces

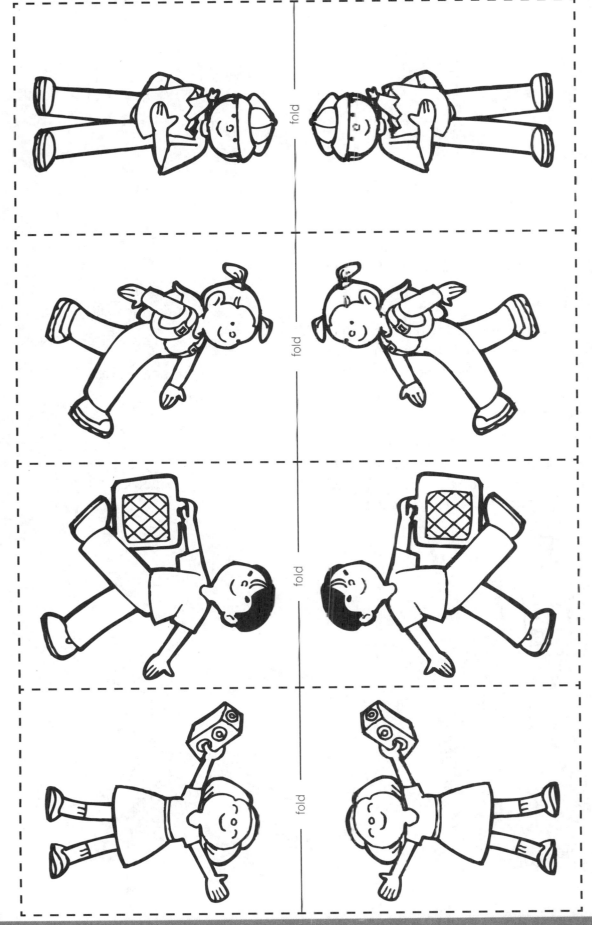

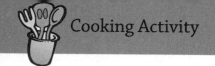
Note: Check for allergies before beginning any cooking activity. An allergic reaction can occur through taste, smell, or contact with allergens.

Neighborhood Trail Mix

Children each bring an ingredient to add to the Neighborhood Trail Mix.

Preparation

1. Prepare a cooking center with all materials assembled.

2. Ask each child to bring in one food item for this cooking activity. Discuss the various food items that can be added to the Neighborhood Trail Mix.

Steps to Follow

1. Each child adds his/her contribution to the large bowl. Each child uses the large spoon to mix his/her contribution in with the other ingredients.

2. Once the mix is complete, spoon a portion into a zipper bag for each child.

3. Eat the trail mix for a healthy snack.

4. Call out the different ingredients as you taste them. Ask the children to raise their hand when you call out the ingredient that they added to the mix.

Materials

- variety of cereals
- pretzels and other crunchy foods
- peanuts and other nuts
- mini marshmallows, small candies
- variety of dried fruits, such as raisins, dates, apples, cranberries, pineapples
- large bowl
- zipper bags
- large mixing spoon

Dear Parent(s) or Guardian(s),

Today we cooked in class. Your child made "Neighborhood Trail Mix." Besides having fun cooking and eating, the children practiced these skills:

- listening to and following directions
- using small motor skills

For our unit *My World*, we will send home a variety of new recipes. Each recipe will be one that your child has tried in class and is excited about. We hope you have an opportunity to try this recipe again with your child. Allowing your child to help you in the kitchen is a wonderful way to reinforce learning skills while creating family memories.

Neighborhood Trail Mix

Materials

- variety of cereals
- pretzels and other crunchy foods
- peanuts and other nuts
- mini marshmallows, small candies
- variety of dried fruits, such as raisins, dates, apples, cranberries, pineapples
- large bowl
- zipper bags
- large mixing spoon

Steps to Follow

1. Add the various food items to a large bowl. Mix after every new item is added.

2. Once the mix is complete, spoon portions into a zipper bag.

3. Eat the trail mix for a healthy snack and call out the different ingredients you taste.

Note: Children draw a line to match each person with items associated with his job.

Name _____

Off to Work!

Draw a line to match.

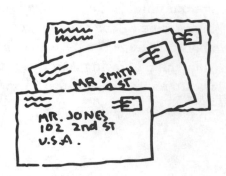

Name _____

Numbers in the Neighborhood

Number the houses.

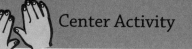

Children match various "tools" with the appropriate neighborhood business.

Materials

- pages 187 and 189
- scissors
- sturdy folder or envelope

Tools They Use

Creating the Center

1. Laminate and cut out pages 187 and 189.
2. Store the cards in a sturdy folder or envelope.
3. Plan time to model how the center is used.

Using the Center

1. Children lay out the four neighborhood business task cards.
2. Children sort the tool task cards into a row under the appropriate neighborhood business.
3. Children turn the neighborhood business task cards over and self-check their answers by matching the colors on the backside of the cards.

Tools They Use

Tools They Use

Tools They Use

Tools They Use

Tools They Use

Tools They Use

Tools They Use

Tools They Use

Tools They Use

Tools They Use

Tools They Use

Tools They Use

Tools They Use

Tools They Use

Tools They Use

Tools They Use

Tools They Use

Tools They Use

Tools They Use

Tools They Use

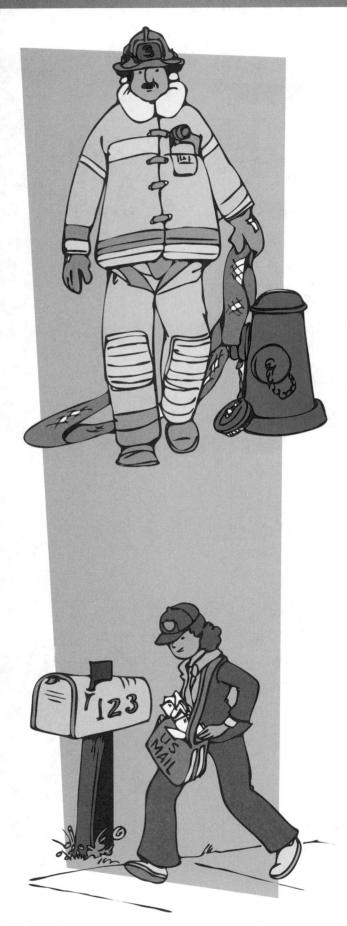

Mr. and Mrs. Friendly's Town Song

Mr. Friendly,
Mrs. Friendly
Live in town
Live in town.
The firefighter helps them.
The firefighter helps them
All around, around the town.

Mr. Friendly,
Mrs. Friendly
Live in town
Live in town.
The police officer helps them.
The police officer helps them
All around, around the town.

Mr. Friendly,
Mrs. Friendly
Live in town
Live in town.
The mail carrier helps them.
The mail carrier helps them
All around, around the town.

Alphabet Cards

Use these colorful Alphabet Cards in a variety of ways. Simply laminate and cut apart the cards and store them in a sturdy envelope or box.

Alphabet cards can be used to practice skills such as:

- letter recognition
- letter-sound association
- visual perception

Alphabet Card Games

What's My Name?   Use the alphabet cards to introduce the names of the letters, both uppercase and lowercase.

Make a Match   Children match a lowercase and uppercase letter. They then turn the cards over to self-check. If a correct match has been made, the child will see a picture of the same object whose name begins with the letter being matched.

First-Sound Game   Use the alphabet cards as phonics flash cards and ask children to identify the sound of each letter.

ABC Order   Children take all of the uppercase or lowercase cards and place them in alphabetical order.

apple

Apple

bedroom

Bedroom

cat

Cat

doctor

Doctor

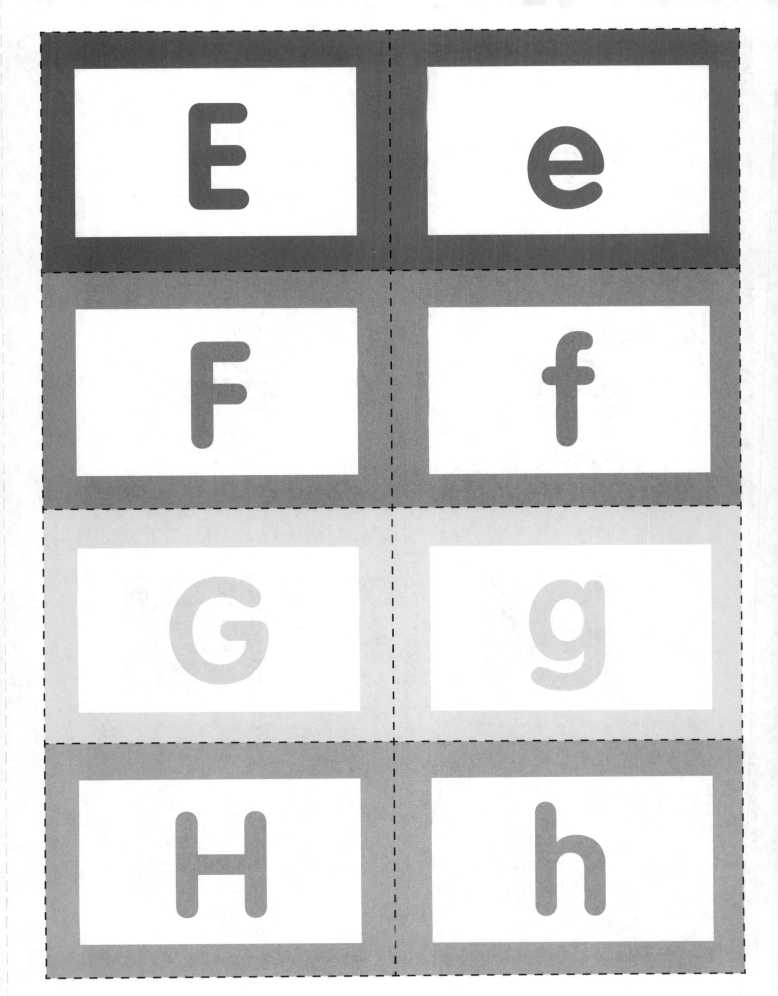

ear

Ear

firefighter

Firefighter

gate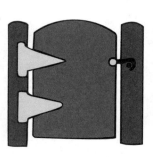

Gate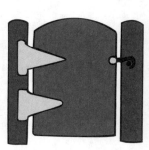

hospital

Hospital

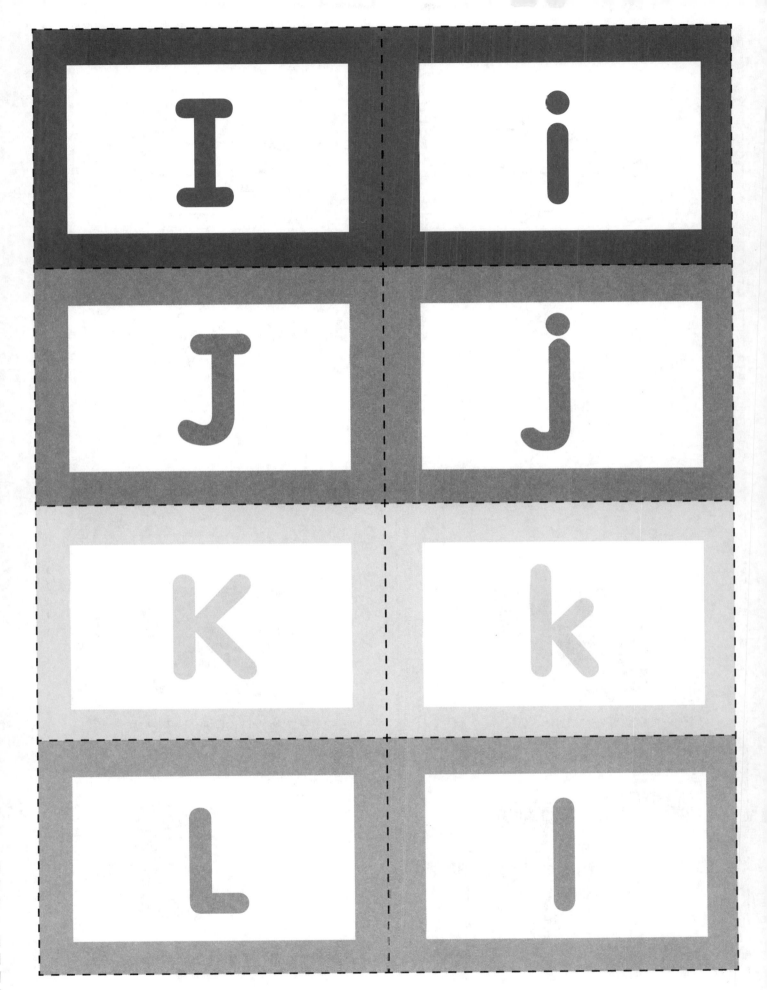

in

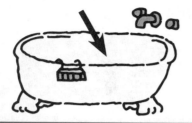

In

jump

Jump

kitchen

Kitchen

library

Library

mother

Mother

nurse

Nurse

on/off

On/Off

post office

Post office

Q   q

R   r

S   s

T   t

quiet

shhhh...

Quiet

shhhh...

ride

Ride

sink

Sink

tape

Tape

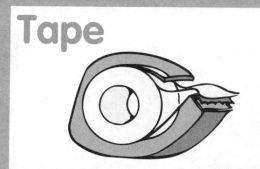

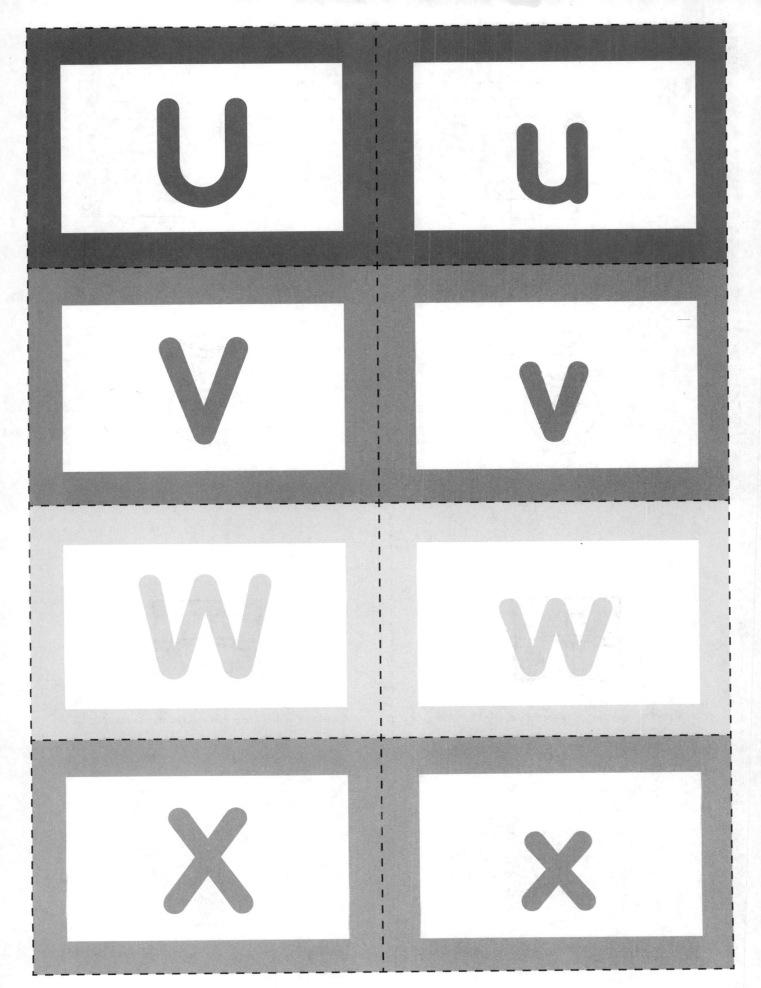

up

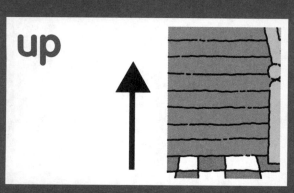

Up

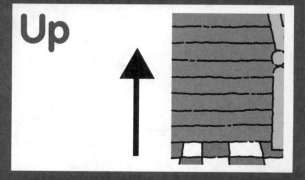

vase

Vase

window

Window

x-ray

X-ray

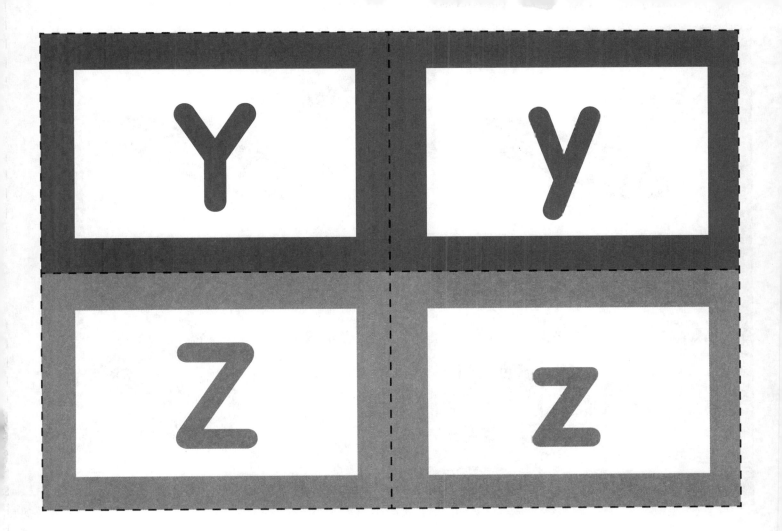

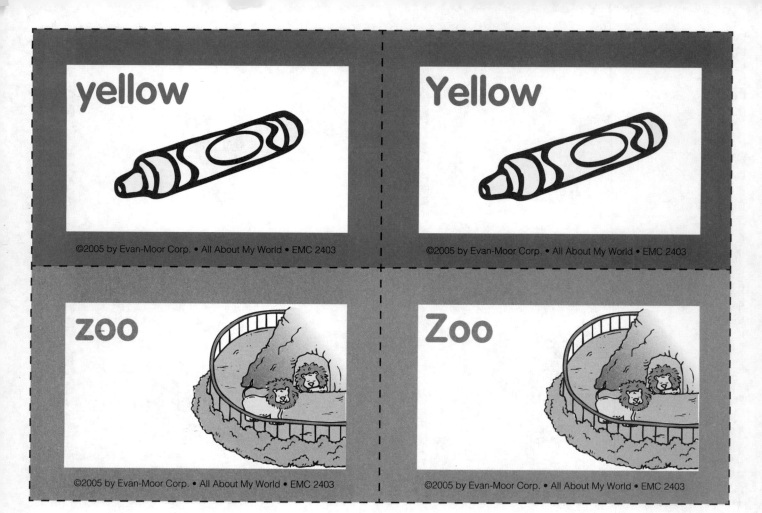

yellow

©2005 by Evan-Moor Corp. • All About My World • EMC 2403

Yellow

©2005 by Evan-Moor Corp. • All About My World • EMC 2403

zoo

©2005 by Evan-Moor Corp. • All About My World • EMC 2403

Zoo

©2005 by Evan-Moor Corp. • All About My World • EMC 2403

Answer Key

Page 28

Page 39

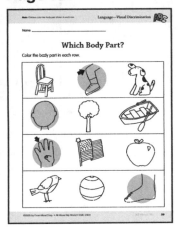

Page 40

Page 41

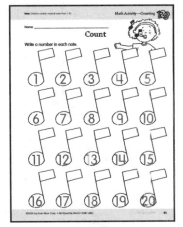

Page 66

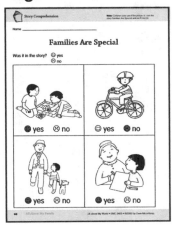

Page 75

Page 76

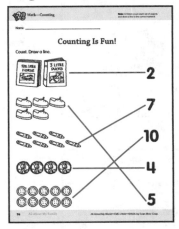

Page 77

Page 102

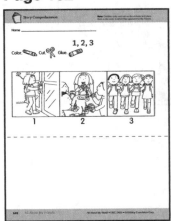

Page 112

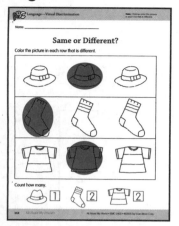

Page 140

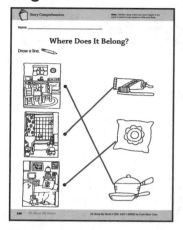

Page 184

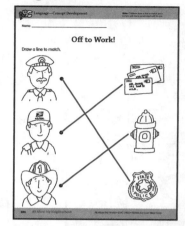

Page 113

Page 148

Page 185

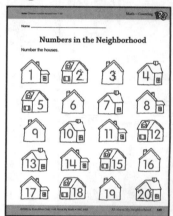

Page 114

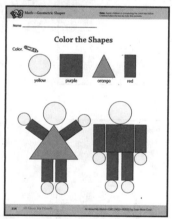

Page 149

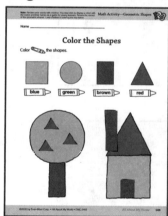

Page 115

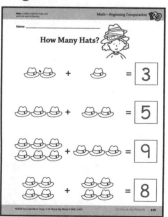

Page 174